The
Great Escape

Also available from Macmillan

THE RHYME RIOT
Poems chosen by Gaby Morgan

THE HORRIBLE HEADMONSTER
Poems chosen by Gaby Morgan

BONKERS FOR CONKERS
Poems chosen by Gaby Morgan

TAKING MY HUMAN FOR A WALK
Poems chosen by Roger Stevens

YOU'RE NOT GOING OUT LIKE THAT!
Poems chosen by Paul Cookson

THE TEACHER'S REVENGE
Poems chosen by Brian Moses

The Great Escape

Poems chosen by
Gaby Morgan

Illustrated by
Jane Eccles

MACMILLAN CHILDREN'S BOOKS

For Grant

First published 2000 by Macmillan Children's Books

This edition published 2003 by Macmillan Children's Books
a division of Macmillan Publishers Limited
20 New Wharf Road, London N1 9RR
Basingstoke and Oxford
www.panmacmillan.com

Associated companies throughout the world

ISBN 0 330 48221 1

3 5 7 9 8 6 4

A CIP catalogue record for this book is available from the British Library.

Printed and bound in Great Britain by
Mackays of Chatham plc, Chatham, Kent.

Contents

Words Behaving Badly

Words
Develop nasty habits –
Getting out of order,
Going off at tangents,
Breaking rules,
Attention seeking.
Give them fifty lines.
They take delight
In ambushing the reader,
Going round in gangs
With their unsuitable friends
Imagining they're poems!
Words –
I'd keep an eye on them
If I were you.

Sue Cowling

The Angel

Last night
I dreamed an angel came
Into our garden,

Blown off course,
From heaven to hell.

Dreamed he took shelter
And slept beneath the apple tree
At the end of the lawn,
His ragged wings wept,
A shroud over his shorn head.

When I woke this morning
I looked across the garden,
And knew that he was dead.

There he was,
Stretched out on the lawn,
Like some great swan.
His head held
Beneath broken wings.

I ran out to check his pulse.
But looking into his eyes
All that I could find
Were the lost skies
Of some distant struggle.

Paler than chalk,
His skin was too cool to touch.
I knew then
That he was dead,

So I stooped
To stroke
His fallen head,

And I kissed his hair,

And as my lips
Touched his cold brow,
And as my kiss
Warmed his cold skin,

Somehow his thin body shuddered
And a glow of heat shimmered
Through his limbs.
Warm and alive
He stretched his wings,
Now no longer ragged,

And his golden laugh
Spilled out across
Our dew-drenched lawn,
Filling that dawn
With a joy that bubbled
Through every blade of grass,
And left the clouds lit
With its own peculiar light.

I dreamed an angel late last night
But now no one believes me.
I keep a feather of bright light
Hidden beneath my bed
Just in case one of my friends
ditches disbelief.
Just in case one of my friends
grows instead
whatever it might be,
that to their cost,
those friends have sadly lost.

Pie Corbett

Routes

1. The Walk to School

Down Barking-dog Lane
past the street with the boat

        Clouds rush by
        Sometimes it rains

Up Old-lady-waving Road
past the field with the car

        Clouds hang still
        Aeroplanes drone

Down Skateboard Steps
past the shop with the cat

        Clouds make shapes
        Reflect in windowpanes

2. The Drive to School

radio shouts
Mum shouts
belt tight
window steam
Dad shouts
radio shouts
feel hot
feel sick
radio, Mum,
Dad shout
shout shout
every day
same shout
same hot
same sick
same same
same same

Ian McMillan

Autumn Gilt

The late September sunshine,
Lime green on the linden leaves,
Burns bronze on the slated roof-tops,
Yellow on the farmer's last sheaves.

It flares flame-like on the fire hydrant,
Is ebony on the blackbird's wing,
Blue beryl on the face of the ocean,
Glints gold on the bride's wedding ring.

A sparkling rainbow on the stained-glass window,
It's a silver sheen on the kitchen sink,
The late September sunshine
Is a chameleon, I think.

Valerie Bloom

Winter Moon

Orange sunset low across the woods
The shock of cold as you breathe in
Daylight gone, the night begins
All too soon the winter moon

Moorhens chatter on the icy lake
A dog patters across crisp grass
Shadows lurk across the path
All too soon the winter moon

Families of mice and voles
Huddle safe inside their holes
Marmalade light yields to the night
All too soon the winter moon

Trees clasp hands, b.
Silent spectral mists advas dance
Distant echoes of a waltz
All too soon the winter moon

Holly and bramble tear your clothes
Someone sleeps with the briar rose
Dark shapes cluster, shadows loom
All too soon the winter moon

Tawny owls wake and shiver
Something makes the branches quiver
Flits across the rising gloom

All too soon the winter moon

Adrian Henri

Cat Message

Shemu the cat
Whose ancestors
Prowled amongst the pyramids
Today received a special visitor

Neferhotep
Ambassador
From the constellation of Orion

Upon Neferhotep's
Departure
Shemu tried her best
To warn her mistress
Of Neferhotep's message

The Earth is about to be invaded

Shemu lay on the carpet
And made letter shapes
With her body
I - N - V - A - S - I - O - N

Shemu brought twigs and scraps of bark
Into the kitchen
Arranged in the symbol O-ki-hran
Which is Orionese for
You are about to be invaded by hideous aliens
From the constellation Andromeda

Shemu even reprogrammed the video
To play Star Trek tapes

But Shemu's only reward
For her efforts
Was some tinned cat-food

Humans, thought Shemu,
Can be so . . .
Dumb.

Roger Stevens

The Snake's Revenge

You could never imagine me,
not in a zillion years,
I'm far beyond the scope of
your wildest nightmares or fears.

But I'm here, at the edge of your universe,
a creature of immeasurable girth.
Hatred has made me huge, and now
I'm the snake that will swallow the earth.

And I'm moving ever closer,
I've already gobbled up stars,
I've unhinged my jaws and soon I'll be ready
to take a crack at Mars.

And when I finally reach you
I'll tell you now what I'll do
I shall wrap my coils round your planet
and squeeze the breath out of you.

And this will be my revenge
from the time that I was cursed,
for eternity spent on my belly,
for the dust that I ate, for my thirst.

And remember well, if you will,
for a snake is nobody's friend,
I was there at the very beginning
and I'll be there at the end.

For the world won't finish in flame
or by drowning in a flood.
It won't be wholly engulfed
in an ocean of angry mud.

There'll be no explosion, no fracture,
no tremors from a last earthquake.
I tell you now, this world will end
in the belly of a snake.

Brian Moses

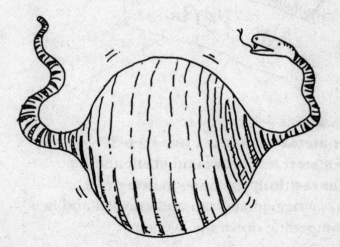

The Great Escape

In the Great Escape from London Zoo
eight caribou and gnu they knew
mounted a minor military coup,
an act of animal derring-do,
and locked the staff they overthrew
in the 'potamus pit and a portaloo,
then caught a plane to North Peru.

Air Peru

As animals broke out two-by-two
to squeal and growl and grunt and moo
a loud unruly queue soon grew
that wriggled and ran and crawled and flew,
stampeding down the avenue.

In the Great Escape from London Zoo
we heard how a herd of kangaroo
had bid the big brown owl adieu
with a: "Toodle-oo, mate, toodle-oo!"
but before he'd time to twit-tu-woo
they'd hopped it, heading for Timbuktu
and the owl himself had flown off too.

While a crocodile and a cockatoo
crossed the Thames in a slim canoe,
rowed by the bird, so the croc could chew . . .
chew through the bones of the eight-man crew
till the river ran red instead of blue.

In the Great Escape from London Zoo
the pandas abandoned their bamboo
and, all dressed up as railway crew,
hijacked the fifteen fifty-two
from platform three at Waterloo
and "parley-voo" they zoomed straight through
Paris, and on to Katmandu.

Panic ensued and ballyhoo
when pot-bellied pig and rare-breed ewe
gatecrashed a very posh barbecue
terribly upsetting the well-to-do
and causing a heck of a hullabaloo.

You doubt my word? What's wrong with you?
Why, every detail here is true.
The Great Escape from London Zoo.
When was that? I thought you knew:
Years ago, at half-past two.

Nick Toczek

We Lost Our Teacher to the Sea

We've been at the seaside all day
collecting shells, drawing the view,
doing science in the rockpools.

Our teacher went out to find the sea's edge,
and stayed there, he's sitting on a rock
he won't come back.

His glasses are frosted over with salt,
his beard has knotted into seaweed,
his black suit is covered in limpets.

He is staring into the wild water
singing to the waves,
sharing a joke with the herring gulls.

We sent out the coastguard,
the lifeboat and the orange helicopter;
he told them all to go away.

We're getting on the bus with our sticks of rock
our presents for Mum
and our jotters and pencils.

He's still out there as we leave,
arms outstretched to the pale blue sky
the tide racing towards him.

His slippery fishtail flaps,
with a flick and a shimmer he's gone
back to the sea forever.

David Harmer

Great Sun

Great sun
Eat the clouds up
So that my love can flourish with my garden,
So that my love, my love
And all the busy joy of greenery
Can flourish.

Storm wind
That brings the clouds
Huge and heavy, stifling up the heavens,
Push on, push them over
So that the flattened garden can be righted
And love recover.

Jenny Joseph

Death Slide

Frozen with fear
I stood at the top,
staring down
at the vertical drop.

My father's voice echoed in my head:
'Be brave, be tough,' he'd always said.

Thirty feet high.
They call it 'Death Slide'.
They said I'd miss out
if I didn't ride.

My father's voice echoed in my head:
'Don't be a coward,' he'd always said.

Pairs of eyes all watch,
waiting for me to go.
It seemed like a lifetime passed
until finally I said, 'No!'

Now there's another voice in my head:
'You're the one who's brave,' it said.

Tracey Blance

Spring Assembly

Right! As you all know,
It's spring pretty soon
And I want a real good one this year.
I want no slackers. I want SPRING!
That's S - P - R - I - N - G! Got it?
Spring! Jump! Leap!
Energy! Busting out all over!
Nothing so beautiful! Ding-a-ding-a-ding!

Flowers: I want a grand show from you –
Lots of colour, lots of loveliness.
Daffodils: blow those gold trumpets.
Crocuses: poke up all over the parks and gardens,
Yellows, purples, whites; paint that picture.
And a nice show of blossom on the fruit trees.
Make it look like snow, just for a laugh,
Or loads of pink candy floss.

Winds: blow things about a bit.
North, South, East, West, get it all stirred up.
Get March nice and airy and exciting.

Rain: lots of shimmering showers please.
Soak the earth after its winter rest.
Water those seeds and seedlings.
And seeds: start pushing up.
Up! Up! Up! Let's see plenty of green.

Sunshine! Give the earth a sparkle
After the rain. Warm things up.

And you birds: I haven't forgotten you.
Fill the gardens with song.
Build your nests (you'll remember how).
And you lambs: set an example,
Jump, leap, bound, bounce, spring!

And kids: ditch those coats and scarves,
And get running and skipping.
Use that playground, none of this
Hanging about by the school wall
With your hands in your jeans pockets.
It's spring, I tell you.
And you're part of it
And we've got to have a real good one this year.

Gerard Benson

Megan's Day

Like any day
I open our front door.
Against the creosote fence,
Above the clustering pansies
The roses glow dull red,
And further off
Beyond the maple
And the overgrown canal
The orphan hill
That has no name
Rises to the blue.

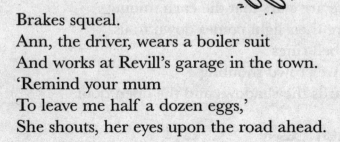

Brakes squeal.
Ann, the driver, wears a boiler suit
And works at Revill's garage in the town.
'Remind your mum
To leave me half a dozen eggs,'
She shouts, her eyes upon the road ahead.

Because it's June and hot today
I sit with Kelly at the back
Beside an open window.
She's not my best friend
But you can always talk to her.
The wind that's blown across the Irish Sea
And half the breadth of Wales
Before rustling our homework books
And my brown hair
Smells hot this day of grass and tar.

Today we're up to Air and Light
In our Jam Jar Science Books.
Later we'll climb on the roof
To drop paper parachutes
On to the playing fields below.
Around the iron gates
The children shout and stare
As we get off the bus.
Next September I'll be at the High School
And someone else
Will sit in my place by the window.
There are stars that die each minute
Before their light comes down to us.
The bell rings
And we crowd shouting
Towards the shadows and the open door.

Gareth Owen

Under My Hair

Under my hair
is a curious place.
It's beneath my skull
and behind my face,

between my eyes
and above my neck,
so look inside,
yes, why not check?

Behind and above
my cheeks and chin,
you're welcome here,
so come on in.

For under my hair
is a curious place,
as, tucked inside,
lies so much space.

But what will you see
and what will you find?
Why, most of me,
my wondering mind:

there are thoughts and dreams
and stories too,
the things I wish
and the things I do.

And whoever I meet,
wherever I go,
whatever I see,
or hear, or know,

gets stored within
this shell so small,
which, strange to say,
can hold it all.

For who would imagine
it might be there,
behind my eyes,
beneath my hair,

where, if you could enter
and look, and see,
you'd get to know,
well, most of me . . . ?

Tony Mitton

Ice Cream

I dreamt of having a dog.
A racing dog.
A chasing dog.
An obedient amazing dog.

I got Scruff.
A rough dog.
A tough dog.
A run-in-circles-and-woof dog.

We were mates.

We liked the same things.
We liked running around the park.
We liked lying around the house.
And we liked eating,
especially ice cream.

We'd tried crisps
but they made him cough.
Shared sherbet made him foam.
Toffee stuck his teeth together.
Chocolate was one gulp and gone.
But ice cream . . .

He'd come running and smack his lips
then he'd be all laps and licks
and wags and shudders and shivers.
He became one huge wag of pleasure.
One excited quiver.

Sounds of bells on Saturday announce the ice
    cream van.
Across the busy street I go, coins hot in my hand.
"Ice cream cornet please – with raspberry sauce."
Then Scruff comes running and smack. Of
    course. A car
Hits him full speed on.

One startled yelp, one shudder and he's gone.
Not the slightest movement now. Not the
   smallest sound.
Ice cream melting on to my foot.
Raspberry sauce sticky as blood.

Michaela Morgan

Mrs Dungeon Brae

Mrs Dungeon Brae lived on the Isle of Mull,
the fairest of the rarest,
of all the western isles,
in a ramshackle farm house,
close to the hoarse heaving sea.

Every morning Mrs Dungeon Brae
was up with her white goats
pulling their teats for thin milk.
If she stumbled across a stranger
on her acre of land,

she reached for her gun, an old
long gun that belonged to her father,
his father before him, his father before him.
Then fired in the fern-scented air;
and watched the crows and stranger scatter.

She laughed a grim dry cough of a laugh.
Her face had all of Scotland's misery –
every battle fought and lost;
but her cheeks were surprises – a dash
of colour, a sprig of purple heather

peeping over the barren hillside.
Once, alone, in her house,
she sat down in her armchair
with her grey hair yanked into a bun
and died –

A tight, round ball of a death.
And nobody found her:
everybody was terrified of trespassing.
So the skeleton of Mrs Dungeon Brae
sits on her favoured armchair,

And the radio is playing Bach.
Ach. Ach.
Mrs Dungeon Brae.
The strings haunting the bones of Mrs Dungeon
Brae.
Ach. Ach. Mrs Dungeon Brae. Ach. Ach.

Jackie Kay

Treat of a Sweet

Jelly A'Quiver shivered a shiver,
when sighting a sight of pure delight:
lollipop slopping ice cream topping.
It splashed it about, shouted a shout:
"A treat of a sweet for all to eat!"
With pineapple crushed, the cherries blushed,
orange segments smiled, peaches went wild,
macho pistachios grew moustachios,
walnuts and peanuts, butt me no buts,
but melt with no trace, fruit and nutcase.

Debjani Chatterjee

The Ascent of Vinicombe

He took his bag off his back and strapped it to his
      chest.
I think this is the start of an adventure, he declared,
and so it was. With great care we roped ourselves
      together,
then slowly, cautiously, we fought our way up the
      ice-cliff.
He led, of course, shouting warnings and
      encouragement as he sprang
from boulder to boulder, dodging avalanches. It was
      hard going.
There was no shelter from the bitter wind and only
      one
lamp-post strong enough to bear our weight. We
      paused a moment
then pressed on, any delay was dangerous. Without
      warning
the pavement would split, opening horrid pits,
      crevasses
crammed with writhing snakes or hairy mammoths.
      Despite it all,
we struggled upwards, risking a traverse of the
      slippery railings,
until we hauled each other, wild-eyed and
      wind-beaten, across the glacier

of Kersland Street. It was then that, with amazing
     speed,
he slipped his coat off and hung it cape-like from his
     head,
announced his possession of super-powers and flew,
     arms outstretched,
up the lane towards the school.

Dave Calder

Before the Days of Noah

Before the days of Noah
before he built his ark
seagulls sang like nightingales
and lions sang like larks.
The tortoise had a mighty roar

RRROAR

the cockerel had a moo

MMOOOO!

kitten always eeyored

eeyore!

and elephants just mewed.
   It was the way the world was
   . . . when owls had a bark
   and dogs did awful crowings
   whilst running round the park.

woof
woof!

whooo!
Whoooo!

Horses baaaed like baa lambs
ducks could all miaow
and animals had voices
quite different from now!
But, came the day of flooding
and all the world was dark
the animals got weary
of living in the ark –

So they swapped around their voices
a trumpet for a mew
– a silly sort of pastime
when nothing much to do.
But when the flood had ended
and the world was nice and dry
the creatures had forgotten
how once they hissed or cried.

So they kept their brand-new voices
– forgot the days before
– when lions use to giggle
and gerbils used to roar.

Peter Dixon

Child With Toy Sword

Clutching in hero hand the bright
Symbol of death and glory,
He marches bravely to the fight
And grows as tall as a story.

The garden birds blow bugles for
His joy as he advances;
The sun declares a playful war
And throws down flashing lances.

And no one whispers to the boy
That some hot future afternoon
He will lunge upward with that toy
And burst the sun like a huge balloon.

Vernon Scannell

Phew! What a Scorcher!

It's seventy degrees:
In the shade
The cat waits to pounce
On dizzy sparrows;
In the sun
The house is undoing its buttons.

It's eighty degrees:
In the shade
The cat pretends to sleep
With one eye open;
In the sun
Tennis players are turning to ice cream.

It's nearly ninety;
In the sun
The grass gets sunburn
And begs the lawnmower to scratch its back;
In the shade
The cat
Sleeps.

David Orme

In Praise of Aunties

An aunt
is a tender plant.
You really can't
be too fond of an aunt.

Judith Nicholls

What's Behind the Stripy Curtain?

"NO! NO! NO!"
That's our headmaster going on and on
at morning assembly in the hall.
Fed up, I stare at the stripy curtain
hanging behind him on the wall.

Behind the stripy curtain
is there a non-smoking dragon
with a code dinnis doze,
or a mini Mercurian
with eyes on its toes?

"NO fighting! NO thumping!
NO punching! NO jumping!"

Behind the stripy curtain
is there an ogre
devouring an ox,
or a fox in a box
in a box in a box . . . ?

"NO kissing! NO shouting!
NO biting! NO clouting!"

Behind the stripy curtain
is there a monster
with worms on its face,
or simply an empty
and echoing space?

"NO running! NO dreaming!
NO spitting! NO screa . . .?"

Suddenly . . . a hand,
a huge, hairy, horrendous hand appears,
grabs our headmaster
and hauls him behind the stripy curtain.
We gaze amazed
then realise he's gone, he's gone for certain!

NO fuss.
NO mess.
He's gone.
We jump up, punch the air,
and shout, "YES!
YESSSSSSSSSSSSSSSSSSSSSSSSSS!"

Wes Magee

A Minute to Midnight

**A minute to midnight
and all is still.**

For example, these are things that are still:
ornaments, coins, lamp-posts,
the cooker, Major Clark's Home for Old Folk

(just opposite our house, which is also still),
the newsagents, a hut, soap, tractors,
freshly ironed trousers draped over the chair.

**A minute to midnight
and all is still
except for the things that are moving.**

Like, for example,
rivers, clouds, leaves, flags,
creaky windmills, lungs, birds' feathers,

digital clocks, grass, the wind,
non-sleeping animals (especially wolves),
planet Earth, the moon, satellites in space,

toenails (well they grow, don't they),
videos that are set to record
programmes in the middle of the night,
washing lines,
mobiles above babies' cots –

and babies' eyelids, they always flicker.

John Rice

Identifying Things

Davy loved natural history –
He wandered round for hours,
Identifying birds and bees,
Identifying flowers.

He knew the names of orchids –
He identified each one,
He identified each butterfly
That settled in the sun.

He knew the names of spiders,
Of beetles, worms and grubs,
He identified the leafy trees,
The grasses, ferns and shrubs.

He knew the names of songbirds,
He identified each tweet –
The wren, the thrush, the wall-creeper,
The ring-necked parakeet.

He knew the names of lizards,
Of snakes and snails too,
He roamed the world, identifying
Species old and new.

Then one day in the mountains
Davy saw something gleam.
He lifted his binoculars
Then gasped . . . was this a dream?

For looking down at Davy
From the canyon's rocky rim
Was a vulture with a telescope –
Identifying him!

Richard Edwards

The Haiku Monster

The haiku monster
Gobbles up the syllables
Crunching words and CHOMP!

The haiku monster
Slurps the 's' in _paghetti
Bites 'b's for _reakfast

The haiku monster
Jumbles all the telrets pu
Makes   disappear

The haiku monster
Nibbles on the v w ls nd
Chews consonants u .

The haiku monster,
Alphabet joker, plays with
The lettuce and worms.

The haiku monster
Hides rude words in the poem
And spoils bum snog vest.

Mixes up the lines
The haiku monster
Ruining all the layout.

Paul Cookson

It's Not What I'm Used To

I don't want to go to Juniors . . .

The chairs are too big.
I like my chair small, so I fit
Exactly
And my knees go
Just so
Under the table.

And that's another thing –
The tables are too big.
I like my table to be
Right
For me
So my workbook opens
Properly.
And my pencil lies in the space at the top
The way my thin cat stretches into a long line
On the hearth at home.

Pencils – there's another other thing.
Another problem.
Up in Juniors they use pens and ink.
I shall really have to think

About ink.

Jan Dean

From a Distance

I climbed to the top of the world today
and the world looked really small.
Guns and bombs and orphan's tears
couldn't be heard at all.
It all looked bright and beautiful
like a cheerful Christian hymn,
with enough green fields and shady woods
to put all the people in.

I couldn't see any fences
or signs which read 'Keep Out';
nor churned up earth where tanks rolled
through
to the enemy's victory shout.
And I couldn't see the eyes of a child
who had no tears left to cry,
or numb refugees at the side of the road
watch the flames from their homes light the sky.

I couldn't see the generals' smiles
as they met to divide up the land,
or hear the lies they told afterwards
with blood still warm on their hands.
I couldn't feel the sigh which leaks
from a million broken hearts
or the thick and sickening silence
before the next war starts.

I climbed to the top of the world today
and dreamed how the future could be:
the rivers unsullied by hatred and greed
and peace stretching clear to the sea.

Lindsay MacRae

Ye New Spell Book

Poems chosen by Brian Moses

In *Ye New Spell Book* Brian Moses has conjured up an enchanting collection of magical verse, including a *Spell to Banish a Pimple*, a *Dragon's Curse*, love charms, old wives' tales and the following sound advice:

On Reflection

Don't practise strange spells in front of the mirror,

don't point at yourself with a wand;

don't practise strange spells in front of the mirror,

I did – now I live in this pond.

Mike Johnson

A selected list of titles available from Macmillan and Pan Books

The prices shown below are correct at the time of going to press. However, Macmillan Publishers reserve the right to show new retail prices on covers which may differ from those previously advertised.

A Nest Full of Stars	0 330 39752 4	£4.99
I Did Not Eat the Goldfish	0 330 39718 4	£3.99
The Fox on the Roundabout	0 330 48468 0	£4.99
The Very Best of Paul Cookson	0 330 48014 6	£3.99
The Very Best of David Harmer	0 330 38190 8	£3.99
The Very Best of Wes Magee	0 330 38192 4	£3.99
Don't Get Your Knickers in a Twist	0 330 39769 9	£3.99
Ye New Spell Book	0 330 39708 7	£3.99
The Colour of My Dreams	0 330 48020 0	£4.99
Are We Nearly There Yet?	0 330 39767 2	£3.99
Taking My Human for a Walk	0 330 39871 7	£3.99
The Rhyme Riot	0 330 39900 4	£3.50
The Horrible Headmonster	0 330 48489 3	£3.50
Bonkers for Conkers	0 330 41593 X	£1.95
You're Not Going Out Like That!	0 330 39846 6	£3.99
My Stepdad's an Alien	0 330 41552 2	£3.99
The Teacher's Revenge	0 330 39901 2	£3.99
Wallpapering the Cat	0 330 39903 9	£4.99
One River, Many Creeks	0 333 96114 5	£9.99

All Macmillan titles can be ordered from our website, www.panmacmillan.com, or from your local bookshop and are also available by post from:

Bookpost, PO Box 29, Douglas, Isle of Man IM99 1BQ

Credit cards accepted. For details:
Telephone: 01624 836000
Fax: 01624 670923
E-mail: bookshop@enterprise.net
www.bookpost.co.uk

Free postage and packing in the United Kingdom